UNDOCUMENTED PRISONER

In Loving Memory of Gloria & Wilson Wilkerson, Melissa Wilkerson, Ray Curry, Dorothy Hodges, Annie & William Turner, Shalmus Curry, Richard Taylor, Tamicka Brooks-Owens, and Randall Parker.

UNDOCUMENTED PRISONER

C. NICOLE

ISBN: 979-8-9871325-2-4

2023912745

Printed in the United States of America

Set in EB Garamond
Designed by Thomas Kneeland

Table of Contents

Dedication

This book is for all the women, men, and children who are victims of sexual abuse and domestic violence who may feel like they can never walk away. I hope you can walk away knowing you are worthy of painless love. This book is for the woman or man who may not feel they have a way out because they do not know their worth. I hope that you walk away knowing that even though you experience the brokenness of another person, you do not have to be broken. This book is for the little boys and girls who experience sexual abuse at the hands of family or friends. I hope they gain the strength to speak their truth early, even when fear arises, and know they are not alone.

INTRODUCTION

I magine graduating from high school and entering your first year of college. An exciting time, one filled with a mix of emotions as you step away from your childhood and toward becoming more. I was the last of the children in the house, finally in school to pursue my dreams of being an attorney. Why? Because I loved debating, research, and it was a passionate hobby. I was a young lady who had what most would consider a lot going for myself. I was still living at home and just enrolling in Purdue University Calumet with my favorite person on the earth, my best friend/cousin—the person I shared my dreams and aspirations with. The both of us were living our dream of working to become college graduates. We had a system where we would take turns picking each other up for school, we made sure to align the majority of classes together because we were first-year students, and we would always stop at Harold's Chicken and get banana pudding and chicken. Harold's was our first spot; Burger King was our second. We longed for chicken sandwiches (the original) and Nestle Toll House cookies. We thoroughly enjoyed the simple things in life. The simple things were about to take a turn. But before we get there, let's talk about how it all started.

Love Doesn't Hurt

Love doesn't hurt are the words
my mother always spoke to me.
I rejected those wise words
because I wasn't ready to be set free.

I thought the fairytale story
would start to unfold if I did everything I was told.
How deliverance took place
& there was no longer a stronghold.

How God set him free and changed his life.
How he became the best husband to his loving wife.
The storyteller had other plans, or he was just that bold.
The only story I was telling was how I ended up in another chokehold.

Gasping for air after being strangled yet again,
just to be greeted with the words,
*if you would have listened to what I told
you to do, this wouldn't be happening.*

Love doesn't hurt, yeah, that's what my mama said;
those were words I heard while dragged out of bed.
Dragged across the carpet as I screamed *please stop it*,
I was afraid for my unborn child, but that didn't stop him.

Sympathy with no empathy because he didn't really care.
It was all part of the manipulation to keep me there.
Love doesn't hurt the words my mother spoke to me
were those I remembered when I was finally set free.

CHAPTER 1:
THE MUGSHOT

On August 14, 1984, one of the dopest human beings was born. I was born in Hobart, Indiana, only because my parents had good insurance, but we lived in Gary, Indiana. I'm sure if you asked my mom, she would say the day I got evicted out of her stomach it was hot and miserable. I am a summer baby. Sorry, Momma, yours and Dad's timing was off. I was the youngest of nine children and, if you could imagine, surrounded by a lot of love. My siblings were a lot older than me except for two. We were not poor, but we were not rich either. We had what we needed and love from our parents. We lived on the East Side of 43rd high school. The neighborhood growing up was decent, but it began changing as we got closer to entering high school. We were unfortunate witnesses to shootouts and drug busts. My parents' white dodge intrepid was shot up after a shootout, and thankfully we had just stepped foot in the house from playing outside. My mother had called us in, and I say God must have put an unction in her spirit because as soon as we came in, gunshots were ringing out. God was watching over us, because we would not be alive if we'd stayed outside.

My parents were both pastors, so it was school, church, and in between we were able to mingle with our friends. We were not allowed to listen to secular music, but of course, we did anyway. I loved music and turned it on when they got out of the car or left the house. My mama always knew though, it was like she could feel the melodies of TLC in the air, talking about 'so I creep.' We could not have playing cards in our house, and my parents ran a tight ship. I did not understand what the playing cards had to do with anything, but it was their house rules. We were like most kids, rebellious to a fault, but they understood because, hell, they were kids before too.

Growing up we were taught the basics in life, but when it came to relationships it was more on a surface level. We did not go beyond the surface and peel back all the layers associated with relationships. I just knew that when I started dating, I wanted a man that had some of the characteristics of my father because he treated my mother like a queen and he made us feel like no one could ever compare. I never heard my parents argue my entire childhood or lift their voices at one another. The thing I saw was the teamwork they had as they navigated all the challenges they were faced with, including mine.

I did not start talking until the age of four years old. My parents did not know what was wrong with me, so they took me to see a speech therapist, who, it turned out, concluded that developmentally nothing was wrong. I just was not ready to talk to anyone, which I totally get now because half of the time people don't listen anyway. I could not imagine how my parents felt, knowing that it was not normal. My parents said that out of nowhere I started talking, and they have not been able to get me to shut up since. Talking was the start of some of the challenges I was soon to experience.

Two years later, at ttehe age of six and up into my teenage years, I was being molested by my then teenage female cousin. We were a close-knit family, so we would be around each other all the time—church, family functions, or just over at the house. She would molest me at my house and at their house. I was a little girl and scared to say anything. I recall the days when my mom would ask me "Why are you chafed?" I would complain about discomfort, but I never had the courage to let her know why. My mother had no indication because that was far from what she thought would be taking place under her roof.

I recall the times my cousin would ask to stay the night or if I could stay the night over at their house. It went from her touching me to her taking my hand to touch her to get off. It started under the covers, then to the closets, where my first experience of oral sex was with a woman. I also was told to perform the act back, which makes me cringe thinking about it. I experienced this for years, but it all ended when I understood that I had a voice to say no. I recall the day my family was made aware. My sister and brother-in-law had a party at their house and stated they needed a sitter for my niece and nephew during conversations. My female cousin stated she would gladly watch them and that was the moment I made my family aware. I was not about to allow my niece and nephew to become a victim of her, so I put a stop to it and used my voice. My mother sobbed at the fact that not only this had happened to me but that it happened under her care and she had no knowledge. I told her it was not her fault; it was my cousin's fault. I believe deep down in my heart that my cousin was either exposed to this by someone she knew or she saw something that she thought was okay and in turn acted

Chapter 1: Mugshot

on what she saw. The trauma a person experiences if they do not heal, a lot of times it is inflicted on others.

My family finding about the secret that I had kept within for many years was the beginning of what I thought was relief for me. I thought I could start healing from the trauma, but I did not know that more trauma was right around the corner, that included a sentencing.

Chapter 1: Mugshot

CHAPTER 2:
THE CRIME

On January 31, 2003, one phone call changed my life. I was eighteen then and became involved in a relationship with a man I had briefly interacted with a few weeks earlier. You may ask yourself what kind of crime I could commit. The crime was a felony of the heart. I began to love someone who was not even capable of loving themselves. How did this happen being raised in a home where genuine love was displayed consistently? Was it because I got caught up, or was my heart too kind? I want to say it was a combination of the two. The thing was, I thought I had this covered, but boy oh boy was I wrong. I was about to learn that what I thought was oh so right was oh so wrong.

The initial conversation was the thing that had me hooked like a fish to a worm. It was the bait being thrown out, and he was waiting for me to bite. If you are a person who likes to fish, you know once you hook that worm, throw it in the water, the only thing left is for the fish to bite. He was this charming young man who had a way with words. He was six foot three and two hundred plus pounds and had just gotten back from the Air Force. He was employed at a restaurant across from the mall and went on about all these things he had going. I was impressed that he had served our country and he had something going for himself. He was intellectually attractive and knew a lot of things. Savvy, with words rolling off his lips like butter on a hot dinner roll. I'm talking about old school rolls in a pack like they used to serve at the church banquets. The conversations we had made me feel seen, as I did not have a lot of dating history because I was only eighteen years old. I had just started dating, having had only

Chapter 2: The Crime

one meaningful relationship, which lasted from 8-11th grade. I thought I was going to be with that person forever, but he was young and had options. I cannot blame him, because I should have been out here on my Dora the explorer shit as well.

I had many people around me who were in relationships, so, naturally, that is something I wanted for myself. My best friend/cousin, who I did everything with, knew I was dating because we always kept each other up to date. She and I were together every day, from riding to school, going shopping, eating dinner, to sharing our dreams and aspirations. I saw how happy she was in a relationship, and I thought I could attain that same happiness.

It was hard for me because of my heartbreak from my teenage love affair; however, I gave him an opportunity to show me who he was. I agreed to go on a double date with him to dinner with my cousin and her boyfriend after he and I went to the movies. To be honest, I cannot recall the movie we went to see. What I do recall is the cologne he had on and how strong it was. I mean he must have used at least half of the bottle because he left my head hurting.

He sat there with his melodic sweet pillar of lies that sounded like music to my ears. Hell, I didn't know he was lying, I was just in bliss. While we were in the movies, he kept trying to kiss me, which I was not completely comfortable with; however, I eventually gave in. I was not used to someone being so adamant about kissing in my past, but I later found out he was skilled at pressuring to get what he wanted.

Chapter 2: The Crime

We left the movies and he proceeded to drop me off at my parents' house. We continued to talk on the phone, but there were no more dates where he had to spend money. I was a young girl who didn't know about expectations from someone you are dating.

Valentine's Day was approaching, but he worked in the restaurant industry, so he could not get that time off. I was fine with that because, let us be honest, it was only a few weeks into our relationship. He was happy too, because he did not have to pay for another date. He told me he had purchased a gift for me and wanted me to come to his job to pick it up. I didn't have a gift at all because let's be real, we had just started talking. I went to the mall and purchased him a gift because I am that type of person. I would not allow a person to buy me something and not do the same. Here I went spending money I did not need to or let alone have. I dropped the gift off to him at work and took my gift out to the car. I noticed there were other bottles of perfume in the car, which he mentioned were for his mother. My first thoughts were, *He is lying through his teeth,* but on the other hand, I hoped he may be telling the truth and those bottles were actually for his mother. I didn't want to focus anymore on that, so I just let it go because it was too soon to be jumping to conclusions.

The time we spent together was made up of meeting up and sitting in the car, riding and talking about life, but I was okay with that at the time because I just wanted to be around him. I have a love for music to the point where I sit and listen to every part of a song, memorize the beat and ad libs. I was like okay, I found someone who has a love for music like me. Yeah, it sounds so minor, but it was major because I was simple-minded.

We continued things the way they were for the next few weeks until he didn't follow through with the plans we had set up. I was getting ready to go to Canada with my parents, as my mother was going to minister at an annual Women's Convention. He was supposed to see me off; however, he was a no-call no-show. I was upset because I hate when people do not follow through and stand me up. He said he fell asleep at his friend's girlfriend's sister's house, and I thought it was strange, but I wasn't going to let that deter my plans. I went to Canada and enjoyed my time, but I would be lying if I said that wasn't on my mind, because I was very skeptical.

I returned from Canada, and we met up, and he apologized for not coming by. I accepted his apology, and we moved forward, but not without a sense of uneasiness on my end. I may not have said much; however, I had taken a mental note.

Time went on and the more we were talking the more he became comfortable, and so did I. The comfort he was experiencing was asking for things without blinking. I know I didn't have kids, but he was asking me for things like I was his mama and he was going back to school. He didn't waste any time and started asking to borrow money. I'm talking about the one thing I was working hard for and didn't grow on trees, yeah, he asked for it. He liked to dress nicely, so he saw an outfit he wanted to purchase along with some shoes from River Oaks mall, so he asked if he could borrow it. I didn't mind but I wanted to be reassured that it was a loan only, as even my own family had to pay me back for loans. I knew his home life situation, which made it easier to believe he needed a loan. He didn't live at home with his parents but with a friend and his mom, so I thought, well, I'll help him out this time. I met him to give him the money and he purchased his items. The time went on and he never gave me my money back, and being the timid person I was, I just counted it as a loss. However, he would tell me he had not forgotten. I do not know how many paychecks he received, but I did not receive one red cent. I soon would discover he was like Tommy from Martin and he didn't have a job. I let it go and just took one for the team because one thing about me is, if someone is down and out, I'm going to make sure they come out on top. I continued with the relationship because I was just helping him out, But letting go was not the best thing to do.

The one time I helped him set the tone for our relationship. A person will only do what you allow, so now he continued to ask for more money. I was under the impression that he was paying his friend's mother, whom he deemed an aunt, to stay with them. The story he painted sounded good, but I later found out it was a lie. I am empathetic naturally, so if you sell me a story, I will believe it. The story he sold was just as good as a New York Times Best Seller, so I felt sorry for him. He could've become a millionaire if he sold that damn story. I became a resource for someone who did not want to be a source of their financial issues. God and Mickey D's should have been his source,

Chapter 2: The Crime

but here I was. Financial issues were not the only ones I discovered. Look here, your girl was not ready.

I recall one day being in the car with him when he received a phone call from a young lady stating she was pregnant. My reaction was calm, but deep down I was boiling like some eggs in a pot, ready for potato salad. I instantly thought, *I know you are lying.* I was more crushed than a cup of ice from Speedway Gas Station on a hot summer day. I didn't think for one moment she was lying, the way she talked to him said it all. The tone of the conversation was more like 'we were kicking it, and I thought you were my boo.' I know how to decipher the way a person speaks. It was nothing casual, and he made it seem that way.

Chapter 2: The Crime

CHAPTER 3: INVESTIGATION

A series of questionable things in a brief period was overly concerning to me but not concerning enough to cause me to stop talking to him. The flags were more than apparent, because they had been thrown out more than a referee at a college football game.

Time went on, and he found himself in a state of not having a place to live. The first thing he did was lean on me, because I had become his resource. He had a sob story as to why he got put out, but I am sure he didn't fulfill his end of the agreement. And now I was complicating my own life for his troubles, because I owed my mother money for a loan for school until my financial aid hit. I was supposed to pay her back, but I did not because I was too busy trying to save someone else when I needed to be saved.

Myrtle discovered I was getting rooms for him because the checking account was in both our names. Clearly, I was not thinking because I know she checked her balance on the regular. She asked me why I was getting hotel rooms, and yes it was over after that. She told me with bass in her voice, "Go get my money out of the bank now." The fear of God had entered my soul because I knew I was screwed and it was time to figure some shit out. I kept trying to push her off, until the day I noticed the money was gone out of the account and she was no longer on it. I was so mad at her. How dare she take the money that belonged to her? The audacity of me, right? I am sure she was madder than I was, but I got over it. The thing I did not do was stop getting hotel rooms for him. I was writing bad checks until they caught on and told me I could not use a check anymore. The checks were bouncing more than a group of kids leaving a party wired on candy. I did it at other hotels until the account was closed. My crazy self was putting myself in a position that could have messed me up for life.

During this time, with everything going on, I started noticing some unsettling things. He was very envious of the relationship I had with my cousin and hated her. We were in a hotel, and he told me to call her, so I did. He started an argument with her and told me I could not talk to her ever again. My cousin was on to him, and she saw straight through the bullshit. He knew that he would lose his safety net if she talked some sense into me. He was in survival mode and would eliminate anything that could get in his way. Flag on the play, I did not realize what was going on, and I went about that night confused. But it was not yet as complicated as it was about to become.

Chapter 3: Investigation

CHAPTER 4:
CHARGING

Chapter 4: Charging

The hotel money ran out, and I was depleted of funds besides the money I had from working, so I helped where I could. He no longer had a place and was crashing at other friends' houses he knew. He would hang out at Tiberon Trails Apartments and play basketball all day and God knows what else. He would keep his belongings in my car, because he was homeless, so where else was he going to put it. I took one of Mama's good comforters out of her house. If she would have known what I was doing, baby she would have knocked me back to 1984 in her womb.

How did I get here? Dating someone homeless but not seeing it that way? I instead was sad for his situation and that someone could be so cruel and put him out. I now know it was not cruelty, it was accountability.

He found out about a vacant apartment in Tiberon Trails, and because he was running out of couches to sleep on he began sleeping in the apartment. We would spend time together during the day at the apartments and at night he would go be a squatter.

One night I was getting ready to leave, and while talking we got in a heated debate and he slapped the shit out of me. I held my face where he slapped me because I was shocked. I froze, and he instantly started apologizing shortly after, talking about he was sorry, he didn't mean to do that. How is it you didn't mean to take your hand, raise, it and go right to the left? My thoughts were all over the place because one, I couldn't believe he did that, and two, I couldn't believe he had done it and gone right to the left? I left, walked into my house, went straight to my room, closed the door, and cried until I fell asleep. I couldn't believe I had become part of something I never envisioned for myself, let alone never witnessed growing up.

My parents were not fighters but lovers. We were taught to love all, not be stupid. I didn't know what to do or say. The one person I would tell everything to, my best friend, I couldn't talk to. I was scared to tell my parents, and as a result, I suffered in silence. It was the second time I experienced something I was afraid to tell someone about.

He reached out to me the next day and asked whether we could talk at his friend's girlfriend's sister's house in person. The same house he'd been at when I went to Canada. But his best friend was there, so I thought nothing of it.

I explained to my friend what happened, and she was ready to beat the brakes off him.

While there, we talked and reconciled because he stated how sorry he was and that it had never happened before, and he was sincere, so I thought. I dropped my friend off and went back home. We continued our relationship, and as time passed, I began to see a disturbing streak in him.

He had anger issues and had a problem with control. If I said something he didn't like we would get into it. We were at the library on a hot day, and to keep his cool we hung out in the car. We were in the back, and we got into it, and that was the second time he put his hands on me. I was once again puzzled and trying to figure out what I did wrong at this point. He apologized, and I forgave him. I dropped him back off again, and he expressed his sincerest apologies, until the following incident.

I would say this became the norm, but one day, I met Lucifer's son. The darkness in his eyes was something I had never seen in my life. We were talking, it turned into an argument, and he got upset with me. He snatched my phone, got out of the car, and threw it up against the apartment wall. I sat there with tears in my eyes at what I had just witnessed. It was like an angry child having a temper tantrum. I didn't have much family history on him but knew he didn't have a good relationship with his parents. I didn't ask the right questions, but honestly, he would have lied anyway. I did find out that he had more issues than *Vogue.*

One day while he was driving my car down Cleveland Street, because of course he didn't have one, we encountered a problem. My parents would have killed me if they knew he was driving my car again, because before, someone had snitched on me and my car was confiscated, so he'd been left to figure it out. We were at a stop sign, and he saw a person he knew behind us in a vehicle. The guy looked like he was out for blood, so he hopped out of the car and started punching him in the face. I was terrified because I didn't know what was about to happen. However, I felt a sense of satisfaction watching him get hit. Sorry but not sorry, because that karma came back and bit that ass. He eventually pulled off after they tussled, but the next thing I knew, he let his parents know and was headed on the first thing smoking to Indianapolis.

Chapter 4: Charging

I should have questioned the fact that he stated they had a troubled relationship, but at the first sound of trouble they helped him flee.

I stayed behind at my parents and continued working while maintaining a long-distance relationship. I was warned when he left by someone to not follow him, but I didn't listen. He convinced me to move down to Indy after a while, because once again he was about to be without a place to sleep again. Cue Kelly Rowland's "Here We Go, Here We Go Again."

The same thing happened, only in another city. I made it my business to find an apartment, so I could be Captain-Save-A-Hoe. Then things transpired faster than a high-speed chase. I was approved for the apartment, put in a transfer at work, and we moved in together. The move to Indy was when the hell on earth began.

Chapter 4: Charging

CHAPTER 5:
INITIAL HEARING

Chapter 5: Initial Hearing

We were now residing together under the same roof. I have never lived with anyone outside of my parents and siblings full-time, so this was all different for me. There was a sense of calmness in the place at initial entry; however, it should have been an indicator the storm was brewing.

I would go to work, he would drop me off, and he would go elsewhere. I started noticing he would talk on the phone and leave for hours with no indication where he was going. Something was off, and so one day I decided to *69 the number, and lo and behold, it was another woman on the other end of the phone. I had a Barbara, this is Shirley moment, and my first question was who is this? The response to my question was "Who is this?' and I already knew what time it was.

I confronted him, and once I did that, he began to strike me, telling me not to question what he does. He also told me not to contact anyone else who called the house or that he called. We had caller ID at this time, so I would see all the women calling, and I was sick to my stomach. He would always start an argument, put his hands on me, and he would with these other women too. The emptiness started kicking in because I was trying to make sure he was okay with housing and money and I was not in my own house. The cycle of him taking me to work while he did what he wanted continued. Then the process of him picking me up extremely late from work started. He wasn't working a consistent job, so he had so much idle time to run the streets of Indianapolis while I tried to stay afloat.

Chapter 5: Initial Hearing

The day I moved to Indy, my car started running hot while on the highway. I kept driving, and when I got there, I went to the gas station. My thermostat was hot, so I let the car sit to cool off. I proceeded driving and kept doing this for a while. I eventually blew the head gasket, and I no longer had an operable vehicle. I had to find an alternative option quick, which I did. I started catching the bus, taxis, and getting rides until I purchased a car, all in a short timeframe. I went to JD By rider, which had to be one of the worst decisions of my life. The vehicle was in my name; however, it was his car, because I had no control. I would have to wait outside at work while my coworker left because he would be late picking me up while out on his rendezvous. I would get into it with him about it, and here we go, another fight where he was beating my ass. The apartment walls were thin; I am sure my neighbors were sick of it. He eventually told me I could no longer use the house phone. I was dealing with him running up not only the cable bill because of him ordering porn, but the phone bill was being run up because of the chat lines he was engaging in. Imagine discovering all this, mentioning it, and next thing you know, the response is a kiss from a backhand.

I was tired of the fighting, so one day, while he left, I packed my stuff up as much as possible in a clothes basket and called my cousin. She came over with a hammer and got me, and we left.

It was the first time that my family was aware of the storm I was going through, and they were all in shock. I was looking really bad, so she made sure to schedule me an appointment to get my hair done and I stayed at her house. He figured it out because I didn't have much family in Indy. He was calling and calling, and he eventually came to her apartment. I know you're wondering how he knew where I stayed, but prior to me moving there I had stayed over at her apartment, and he ended up coming over and staying as well. He knocked on the door and kept knocking and stayed in the hallway for some time. He kept calling, and after a few days I gave in and answered the phone. He convinced me to come back, and I did and left without a trace.

I eventually talked to my cousin, and she was not happy at all with me, but I needed to get my belongings from her place. She met me outside and shared choice words with him and stated, "I'm not her, and I will kick your ass." She was in absolute tears. I got my stuff and left while hanging my head low. We went back home and acted like everything was okay. The fighting started back up immediately and, in that timeframe, my vehicle got repossessed with all my belongings in it, all while facing eviction. My world was falling apart right before my tear-filled eyes, and I felt like there was nothing I could do. Life was moving at a pace I could not handle. We ended up staying with someone he knew, and that person allowed him to use his car, so at times, I could have a ride to and from work.

We stayed there for a while and started looking for a bigger apartment to share with her and split the rent. It was going to be a win-win situation, until we had an incident. We played in the hall of her apartment, and he became serious, put me in a chokehold, and I couldn't breathe. I instantly got upset, and we got into it. I told our roommate about it, and she said something to him. She was against what he did and tried to defend me, but he told her to mind her business. I went to the mall with her to get my eyebrows done the next day, and all hell broke loose. He got upset, and she told him he was trying to control me, which he was. The argument ensued, and it got horrid quickly. When he got angry, it was like he was overtaken by something and would black out. He grabbed a knife, slashed her tires, and busted out her back window. I remember her trying to stop him, and he pushed her in the process. I was in utter shock because although I saw how ugly he could be to me, to see it happen to someone else messed me up. It was not just me; he had no respect for anyone and would hurt anyone he could not control. We left and were faced with having nowhere to go.

We were beyond broke and now homeless. He reached out to a friend of the person he had committed the offense against, and he took us to a hotel room and paid for it. We had to figure it out at that point, but it was nothing to figure out when you do not have any resources. We ended up at Marsh on West 38th street, where I had to make the call I never thought I never would, calling the only people I knew who could help me. My parents. I had to sleep in a stall that night in the grocery store, one of the nastiest places ever. However, I needed rest because I was mentally and physically drained. The very next morning my dad, brother, and brother-in-law drove to Indy to rescue me. The type of parents I have are amazing, because in their hearts, knowing what he had done to me, guess what—they allowed him to get in the car and go back to Gary where his family was.

The ride was not pleasant at all. My brother, who was a Marine Vet, was ready to annihilate him in the car that day. An argument ensued and my dad had to tell them to cut it out. I will say it was the worst two-hour ride I have ever experienced. But we finally made it.

CHAPTER 6:
DISCOVERY

Chapter 6: Discovery

We arrived in Gary, and he had no place to go. My dad dropped him off at the Village Shopping Center so he could figure it out, because hell would freeze over before they let him in the house. I recall my parents getting him a hotel room, though they were in no financial position to help him. He did not have anywhere to go but the heart my mother had, she ended up reaching out to a shelter, and he was able to stay there. My parents were not aware of what had transpired as far as all the other instances of fighting down in Indy; I never followed up with them. I am sure they would never have done what they did if they had been aware. The only thing they knew was that their baby needed assistance, and they would make sure I got it. He would come over to my parents' house, walk all the way from the shelter, and spend time there. He was fed, clothed, and even given money. I found a job working at Americall, and soon enough, I was able to find a car.

I moved out of my parents' house, and we moved into an apartment complex in Merrillville. It wasn't long after we settled that the drama came. I was finding numbers in his pockets, his male friends were coming in the house at all hours, and the lack of being picked up from work started again. He would either fall asleep or not show up. I would often have to call my parents, or there were times when coworkers would take me home. It was a pattern starting over with other women and back to the fighting after being confronted. The disrespect was at an all-time high, and he wouldn't pick me up for many days. Finally, the inevitable happened and we lost our apartment. I still do not know the truth about how he obtained the apartment, probably with his mouth full of lies. I am unsure if losing it was a combination of the lease not being paid and the altercations, but again, we were homeless.

We had to sleep in the car, and I was not able to allow my parents to know what was going on with me. My parents were pop up parents, and they found out I was lying to them, telling them I had somewhere to stay when we did not. My family was following me, so I'm sure they were alarmed by my state of living and choices. We would get hotels when we could and sleep in the car when we couldn't afford it.

During this time major things happened. The first was while staying in a hotel we got in an argument. I had never fought back any time he would put his hands on me, but I did that day. He hit me, and I punched him in the middle of his "Helmet Head" as hard as I could. I do not know why I did that, because, baby, he took his hands, wrapped them around my neck, and strangled me. I could not breathe and had a panic attack. He drove me from Merrillville to Gary to my parents' house and told them he didn't know what was happening to me. If my dad had known the truth, the results would not have worked in his favor. My parents got in their car, and I rode with him. The entire ride, he told me I better not say anything. We went to the ER, and I was discharged after no findings.

My dad knew what was going on without me saying anything. We went back to the hotel and later that night he apologized, only to follow up with wanting to have sex.

Time went on and we were still in and out of hotels. In the period of homelessness, he got a phone call. The phone call was from his friend's girlfriend's sister. She called to let him know that she had a baby and it was his child. My mouth dropped once again, like, "I know you lying." I started doing the math, and lo and behold, it was when I went to Canada. He was cheating on me and that is why could not come to see me leave. I tell you what is done in the dark always comes to the light, and that light be bright as hell. He now had two kids, a few months apart, and the reality was—I was not going to leave him. I had to figure out how to cope with yet another child in the picture. We had started visiting this church where he knew the pastors, and he eventually started doing some work. They helped him get some form of employment. We had a cover for the windshield, and we would bathe wherever possible. I recall him going out of town for work to paint, and I had to go stay with my parents.

After not having somewhere to stay, we finally got an apartment. I was working a job and taking free CNA classes. I was working nonstop and was getting little to no rest. The car I had eventually got repossessed, so I had to figure out what to do next. I went to a buy-here, pay-here lot and purchased a vehicle with the help of my parents.

The thing is, he hated my parents, but when it was beneficial for us, he would tell me to ask for their help. It was by any means necessary for him. He was able to acquire a job at the steel mill, but after the drug test came back, he lost that job, at a time when they were paying good money, so I was back to being the breadwinner. I ended up getting a second job at a nursing home and quit the other job after working them both because I was tired. I would work and go home to a house full of hell. The same behaviors were happening, and the fighting progressed. It was like the more I worked the more we fought. He would still be talking to other women; I would confront him and start an argument, which led to fighting.

During this time, he attempted to be an active parent in the child's life he had by his friend's girlfriend's sister and tried to be active in the other child's life, but that didn't work out because they were not civil with each other on his behalf. I had to be mature about it because, let's be real, the child was not the problem, it was their father. He gave me a glimpse of the type of parent he would be, and that glimpse was not good. He got his daughter a few times but he always would get into with her mother, so he stopped getting her.

I felt like he took his frustrations out on me. The fighting became more intense and was different than normal. It had gotten to the point where it was moving beyond the slapping and punching, he was treating me like I was another man. He stopped wanting to take me to work in my car, so he told me I needed to find another way. I reached out to my coworker, who I knew lived by us, and she would pick me up. There were times when I couldn't go to work because I was so bruised, but I couldn't let her know. She would knock on the door; sometimes he would answer and sometimes he would not. It was pure turmoil.

Chapter 6: Discovery

I eventually revealed to her what was going on, and I would escape for the second time in less than two years. I involved my parents without them knowing. I told them I needed to go to Saint Anthony to get my certificate of completion so that I could take my state boards. He knew they were going to take me. He didn't know that I had plans to leave his ass. I got in the car, and that is when I told my parents I was leaving. I left without anything because those material things didn't matter to me. My parents immediately helped me and got me out of town to Muncie as soon as possible

I ended up at my sister's house in Muncie to start over. I found peace in reading her collection of Eric Jerome Dickey books. I had it made up in my mind that I was done and was never going back. My family made sure I had clothes, got my hair done, and the things I needed. The look in their eyes said they believed me this time. I found a job working at the Gap store in the mall. He was reaching out and reaching out and reaching out and reaching out, but I was remaining strong. I ended up purchasing a vehicle at yet another buy here, pay here place in town.

Time kept going by, and I finally folded. I realized it was harder to go through the healing, so I always relapsed, because I believed his lies. He would say I'm gonna change, and God wants us to be together. Lucifer was working more overtime to get me back than he could on a job he kept for two hot seconds. I eventually left Muncie and went back to Indy without a trace. My family was constantly hurt and disappointed, and I didn't want to feel the hurt. I became toxic to those around me.

CHAPTEr 7:
PLEA BARGAINING

Chapter 7: Plea Bargaining

I returned to Indy with no plan in mind, and he didn't have one either. We just knew that we were going to figure it out. We had no place to stay but we both found a job. I was working in a warehouse, he found a job at Labor Ready, and eventually landed a job as a maintenance technician. He lied on that application like he always did when he would find a job. We were sleeping in the car and bathing at gas stations. The local Shell gas station became my bathroom, and I would cringe whenever I opened the door. I would have never thought I would be in the place I was, but I was doing it all to be with him. The apartments he was working on were vacant, so we sometimes slept in them. I had become a squatter just like him. We would stay at hotels in between and sleep in the car at other times. I recall when we would sleep in the car in the sweltering heat and mosquitoes would feed on us. It was so bad, and I was miserable or "Stuck on stupid and parked on dumb." The windows would fog up, and people coming out of their apartments would see us sleeping in the car. I was at a low point, but not as low as I was about to feel.

We were outside a hotel one day because we didn't have any money, so we were in the car. He told me he was going to get some money from this young lady he knew to borrow. I came to know it was a young lady he had met after I left him in Merrillville that he began living with. I believe he had to be dealing with her prior because how did he have somewhere to stay so quick. I have never seen a man that could get things from women like him. I was okay with it because at this point, I needed somewhere to stay. I remember they ended up getting into an argument and she said she was going to get the money to him.

I was allowing him to use another woman so I could benefit from it. I had hit an ultimate low. I had picked up his survival methods and was willing to use whomever to get what I needed. He would get out of the car and talk to her, and I was noticing it and the questions started. He was in a relationship with her and me at the same time and was playing us both. I really got played because it was revealed that she was in fact pregnant. I was like, *geez*, this isn't happening *again*. The thoughts in my mind were torture, like how he keeps having babies on me. The timeline didn't add up with this child either, so I instantly became agitated when I heard the news. I went into silence with him because there was nothing to discuss. He called her back, and they continued talking, and I eventually went to sleep.

The next few weeks we ended up finding an apartment. He did the process and I corresponded over the phone. I was not able to physically see it because I had to work. He handled everything, and I just went to sign the lease. We got the keys, and the apartment maintenance guy kept trying to say to get the apartment on the other end. I didn't understand what he was saying at the time. I was like, man, I need somewhere to lay my head, we don't have time for this. I wish I took heed to what he was trying to convey to me, but I found out very quickly.

We opened the doors to the apartment, and I was so excited until I smelled something that would make you cough. The smell was familiar, but I couldn't put my finger on it until I walked in the kitchen. My mouth dropped as I saw the roaches on their backs sunny side up on the counters. I mean, there were plenty of them, and I could only imagine, as they were going to roach heaven, singing "Another One Bites the Dust." It was bug spray I was smelling, because they had fumigated the place. It all clicked; the man was trying to warn us the apartment had several guests that were not on the lease. I could only think of the movie *Joe's Apartments*, and my skin was crawling.

It was too late at this point, because we needed somewhere to stay. I was so disgusted, angry, frustrated, traumatized, and disappointed. I was afraid to sleep, and for the first few weeks I would stay up until my eyes would not allow me to do so. The roaches were active, and it was an infestation. They would come out for breakfast, lunch, dinner, and snacks. I felt like I was calling the kids out of their rooms to eat. We tried to plug up all the holes in the apartment to minimize them, but that didn't work. Growing up, I heard roaches only came out at night, but I found out that was a lie. We hadn't ever had them, but a family member did. I stayed at their house once, and never again. I was not about to let them have a field day crawling on me while I was trying to get some rest. I was always on edge in this apartment, but I had to stay there.

While there, I ended up switching jobs and working at a place downtown. In the process of it all, the car I had ended up getting repossessed, so now I was back to not having a vehicle. I was catching the bus and eventually found a service that would drop me off at home at night.

Chapter 7: Plea Bargaining

We were settled in this apartment and the fighting just carried over. We got in an argument and the next thing you know I was going through the drywall. The imprint of my frail body in the wall, and once again he apologized after and wanted to have sex.

The talking to other women on the phone and on chat lines, running up cable bills watching porn, and having women pick him up continued. I didn't know he was being picked up until the investigator in me kicked in. I watched him one night as he left. He acted like he was going to one of the guys' places in the complex; however, he had a young lady who picked him up. I sat and waited for him to return. He came in the door, and I asked who she was, he lied, and I tried to run out the door to confront her. I was stuck on stupid and parked on dumb. I tried to run down the stairs, and he was pulling me back. He beat my ass after, called her, and they laughed in my face. He told me she would have kicked my ass had she got out of that car. I didn't know if that young lady had a gun or not, but what I was not going to do was let her embarrass me all the while he was. He then, after this, wanted to have sex. It was a pattern of this, and I was going to work with bruises and lying to my coworkers. He wasn't working, and I was back to being the only income earner.

I came home one day and there was a red envelope on the door, and lo and behold, it was a sheriff's notice. I had no clue he had not paid the rent, but what I now knew was we had to be out of there in a matter of days. We packed up and called a taxicab to stay at a hotel in Speedway. We stayed in the hotel, and I continued working, but my job assignment had ended, so I had to find another job, which I did quickly. I started working at Covance while living in the hotel and he got a job at a dealership. I would catch the bus to work, and because he was at a dealership, he would sometimes drive the cars home.

We eventually moved into the apartments next door. I was still catching the bus, and one day, I saw my cousin while at the bus stop. She picked me up and took me to get Burger King before dropping me off. The cousin who picked me up is the same one who came and got me the second time I escaped. I called him to let him know I made it and he asked me how I got to work so quickly. I told him over the phone, and I already knew what time it was. He was waiting at the door when I got home to beat the brakes off me and told me to never talk to her again. He was so controlling; I was required to call him when I got to work and left. I started catching rides with my coworker until we went and purchased a car from another buy here, pay here dealership. He was working at Hare until they found he had a driver's license that was suspended. He had a few good weeks that he was able to finesse out of them. He lost the job and I'm thinking *here we go, here we go again.* I was so right, because the only thing that changed was our location.

He didn't stop putting his hands on me, instead he kicked it up a notch. He was still dealing with other women, one of whom was his ex-girlfriend. I remember going to work and coming home smelling Victoria Secret bubble bath, and I was like *what is that?* The thing about fragrances, if you don't wear certain ones, you will smell them instantly. I asked him what the smell was and he denied it, making it appear like I was crazy. I found it behind the bed, which made me look further. I opened the left bottom drawer and lo and behold, I found a towel and a magazine, along with lotion. I confronted him and that was when he kicked it up a notch on the pain he was about to cause. He broke a vessel in my eye and busted my lip; this was all before I went to work. I went to work and lied to my coworkers and said I slipped and fell. My one coworker said, "I don't believe you, but if you say so." The constant lying became the norm for everyone.

We continued to stay in that apartment until it was eviction time, but that didn't come before Rent A Center came and repossessed all the furniture while I was working. The cycle of losing everything just was continuing. The vehicle ended up repossessed and we were headed back to the hotel.

We went and stayed with a family member of his in her beautiful home. I was reluctant, but the offer was extended, and it was an opportunity to get back on our feet. We stayed for a while, and I thought us being there would bring me some peace, but there is no peace when you are living with the devil. I just hoped that the beatings would stop; however, he didn't care. He had become more controlling and didn't want me interacting with anyone in the house, I think because of the fear of me telling. While living there, one day we got into because he was stating that I was gay because of me being molested as a kid. He forced me to call the person who had molested me to ask why they did it. I was not ready to discuss that; however, I had no choice. I was beyond upset in that moment and I had to sit in my thoughts while he left the house after.

The person we were staying with often would allow him to use her vehicle to get me from work at times, but most times I would have to catch the bus. I eventually started getting rides to work with one coworker and gave her gas money. I was required to let him know when I made it to work and when I was headed home. He would clock me, and if I didn't make it home within the time allotted, I had to suffer the consequences. My face would greet the floor and my lips would tongue kiss the carpet. He would accuse me of cheating on him and being disrespectful to him. I would say I can't control how people drive, but he didn't care. He was looking for a reason to hurt me.

There was someone else living in the house with us and she confessed to me she knew what was going on. I talked to her and cried to her. She let me know that she witnessed him talking to other women and he tried to make it appear she was crazy. I was so miserable staying there when I really thought this would be a moment of refuge, until I went to the next hell destination.

I remember being at work and noticing I had missed my period. I took a test in the bathroom, and lo and behold—a positive test. I was happy because children are a blessing, but I felt empty. I got pregnant when I thought I could not, and, in full transparency, I had tried to get pregnant.

I let him know, and he appeared happy, but let's be honest, he was a great actor. I scheduled an appointment, only to find out I was two months along. It was time to now find our own place, because the room we were occupying was not going to work. We ended up staying there for a while until he got into it with the person we were staying with, and we had to find somewhere to go. We found a house to rent in the hood, and it was decent.

Chapter 7: Plea Bargaining

CHAPTER 8:
PRELIMINARY HEARING

Wgo moved into the house on Udell, and it was nice and spacious. Just what we needed for a newborn. I figured out which buses I would need to utilize to make sure I was able to get to work. I did that for quite some time, until we got a car from my parents. The same pattern just in another place, but this time there was a twist. I was pregnant, so my mind and emotions were changing. I was no longer thinking about myself but about the child I was carrying. The concern I had for myself took a back seat for the concern of my unborn child. I noticed that I began protecting my stomach while he would hit me. He didn't care that I was pregnant, it was like something was just brewing in him.

We were fighting a lot more than ever, and it got bad. He took a speedway size cup of water and poured it on me and slapped me in the ear and jumped on top of me. He would just start the arguments, beat my ass, and leave. He had a pattern, which meant it was another woman. The women I did not know about but somehow speculated because he would come home and make a phone call as soon as he got there. I knew what he was doing, just letting them know he had made it safe. I stood at the top of the stairs, and that is when I heard him. I kept it to myself because I knew where it would lead. I was trying to limit any more trauma to my body that was now housing an innocent human. He wasn't worried about making sure the innocent human was okay, because he would wake up in a rage. The devil must have been talking to him in his sleep, because that demon was brewing. He woke me out of my sleep in the middle of the night and dragged me out of bed. His eyes' blackness was resemblant to what you see in movies, and he looked possessed. He accused me of cheating on him and started hitting me. He proceeded to drag me to the closet door and slammed the door on my leg. He dragged me without remorse and told me to shut up. The same morning, he apologized but with a threat. He had a piece of metal that was a car object, and he threatened me with it. He said he would not have to hurt me if I just listened. I went upstairs and went into the room and cried my eyes out.

It was around the Christmas holiday, and we were going to visit family in Gary. He was locking up the house and I saw a card in the back seat. I read it and it was a card from a lady who he was seeing. I had seen a KFC cup in the kitchen a few days prior with burgundy lipstick on it and said something about. He told me not to worry about what he does and threatened me. It was the one time he did not put his hands on me. The card, however, was wishing him a Merry Christmas from her and her daughter. The kicker was I was experiencing itching that was very painful in my vaginal area. I was utilizing Vaseline because I thought I was experiencing some mild irritation. We got to our destination, and I crossed my legs, hands in my pocket, scratching unnoticeably. I was ready to pull my hair out of my head and detach my vagina from my body. I had to get a cold towel because the feeling was unbearable. I'm grateful I had a doctor's appointment scheduled for that next week.

I told the doctor what was going on, and she said congrats, you are having a boy. I was happy; however, she said we needed to check to see what the itch was about. I looked at her and she said, "You have Trick," and I went blank. I was like what is that? She explained it was a sexually transmitted disease called trichomoniasis that men get from sleeping around. My mouth dropped and she instructed me it would be okay, and it is curable. She prescribed medicine for me and him, because he would need to take it as well. The crazy thing is, a friend of mine who lived around the corner had mentioned she had it and I had questions after that but never mentioned it to either one of them. I'm not saying they were messing around, however I do know he was getting weed from her, so maybe that wasn't the only thing they were passing around.

The trick gave me Trick and I was now to make him aware. I thankfully had gone to the doctor's appointment from my sister's house, because she dropped me off. I went to her house after and called to let him know. He went off and told me I better get home immediately. He called me a trifling bitch and accused me of sleeping around. We argued on the phone, and I let him know I was going to miss the bus, so I had to stay over at my sister's house. My sister was not taking me home after he acted a fool. I caught the bus the very next morning and he was waiting for me in the kitchen. I could not get in the house before he said, "You gonna quit lying to me. Who have you been sleeping with?"

I said, "Nobody, I would never cheat on you, and furthermore I would never put my child at risk." He struck me continuously and called me a nasty hoe. He told me he knew I was sleeping around and was more than convinced in his twisted mind. I went upstairs and showered so that I could get ready for work. I was so crushed that he would try to accuse me of something he was doing.

We made up after that and moved forward.

Shortly after this we would get in a car accident by an uninsured motorist. I was uninsured as well, because let's just be real, I didn't have the money for a car and insurance. We eventually could not drive the vehicle anymore, so here we were, back to not having an operable vehicle. The house we were in had an infestation of mice, which the property owner was trying to manage, but it was not manageable, so eventually he stopped paying the rent and we had to vacate. I mean, *another* eviction, and this time it wasn't just us two, it was the three of us. We had to move quick, so we found an apartment, got accepted, rented a U-Haul, and moved. I was five months pregnant, carrying a desk up a flight of stairs in dead smack winter. What was I thinking? I wasn't. I just knew if I didn't do what I was told, there would be consequences.

We were all moved in, and it wasn't long before he started becoming friends with people in the neighborhood and his ways were displayed. We were struggling financially because I was missing more work due to being pregnant and developing sciatica, so I had to go to therapy. I was working twelve-plus-hour shifts, big belly and all, to stay afloat, or so I thought. My ex was not going to work, but he was gonna steal some groceries. There were times when we didn't have food, so I was a pregnant woman who was starving. I had people at work who looked out for me.

He didn't care because he didn't have to work for anything. I worked until the day before I had our son because I couldn't afford to miss a day. Our son was born, and I brought him home, and it went downhill.

The cycle of not paying bills was still going on, and the lights got cut off a few days after the birth of our son. My son and I stayed with my sister while he stayed behind until the lights got turned back on. It was these moments when I said this child is not going to make him change his ways, and I was right. Shortly after the lights were back on, we ran into a bigger issue. My rescuing cousin's neighborhood had a garage sale, so she invited myself and my mother to go with her. My cousin bought a matching stroller and car seat for my son, and other things. We left and went home, and as soon as I could get in the door, he started an argument. He told me and the baby would need to sleep in the other room that night. He said the baby was not his due to his light complexion and his blue eyes. I told him that was ridiculous because he looked like him. While arguing, he told me he would throw us over the balcony, and I believed him. He proceeded to strangle me and immediately after he left.

I had left the car seat in my parents' car that my cousin had bought, so they came back. I tell you what—God always knows when to come to your aid. My parents came and I immediately told them what transpired. My dad put the chain on the door and that is when I met Lucifer's son. He broke the chain after he realized what was going on. He charged after me and my parents. My dad is not a spring chicken, so he pushed my dad down and tried to snatch our one-month-old child who had no neck stability out of my mom's hands. The next thing I know, my sister and brother-in-law were coming through the door. He punched my sister in the jaw and my brother-in-law had withdrawn his gun. The two began to fight and he was about to throw my brother-in-law down the stairs; however, at this point the police officers were running up the stairs. He was arrested immediately, and a victim advocate came out to the house. I left and went to my sister's house, who lived around the corner. I went there to figure out what my next move was going to be.

He was locked up, so I returned to the apartment and grabbed some of our belongings. My son and I eventually went to my parents' house back in Gary. I wanted to make the best decision, seeing my son was only one month old and I could not make sense of what was going on. The severity of what happened hit me, because many people could have lost their lives that were important to me. My parents got us new clothes and got my hair done.

He must have figured out that I was at my parents' house because he started calling their house non-stop. He had an active protective order against him, yet he chose to violate it and contact me when he was not supposed to. The incident was the first time that he was reported for domestic violence. I had never called the cops in the many years and times I was attacked. He kept calling and I kept ignoring, kept calling, kept ignoring. I eventually gave in and found myself in the basement sneaking talking to him on the phone. I was trying to fight the feeling, but he was wearing me down and I was sick of being without him. It is crazy after what he had just put me and my family through, yet I was sick about not being with him.

He ended up talking me into getting back with him, and I fell for it again. He got out and was put on house arrest. I found myself in courtrooms now, asking for protective orders to be dropped. Why? Because I wanted to be back with him. The apartment had not been paid, so he got evicted, and when he got out of jail, he was staying with a young lady in the same apartment complex. He stated he was not dealing with her, yet she was upset with me and one day decided to call and tell me everything. She stated they were sleeping together, which he claims they were not. She threw all his stuff off her balcony when she found out he was talking back to me. It was a whirlwind of foolishness occurred and the next thing you know she was calling the cops. I was still in Gary at this point, and he ended up in violation of probation because that is what he was given for my case.

He was controlling me from the jail cell. He would want me at the house when he called and if I weren't he would get upset with me. My parents knew I had fell back again, but they were not going to let me out in the streets. They just had peace knowing that I was in the house with them, protected.

I had so much help and support from family while back home. I was able to raise my son while not having to work. I eventually got a job in 2008, against my parents' will. My parents knew that if I got good on my feet, I would be back out the door. I didn't get it during that time, but I do now. I had someone to take me to an interview and I was hired. Dad was not going to take me to work, period, and I do not blame him. I went into survival mode, developed a game plan, and I caught the bus and taxicabs from the point the bus line stopped. I eventually found childcare, where the lady provided transportation. I really felt like things were looking up. He got out of jail and ended up coming back to Gary. The childcare ended on his account, and I had no say so. He ended up sending our son to the daycare at the church where he had worked at one point in time. He stayed with a friend for a little bit of time, but he had a girlfriend, so his time there was short lived. We ended up staying in a hotel that I now know had bed bugs. I would wonder why I was feeling bites all over me and could not figure it out. I thought bed bugs were a myth, but clearly they were the truth.

He ended up getting two jobs, one at Portillo's and the other at Cinnabon, and that was the longest he kept a job until he got fired from both. I was glad he got a job at Portillo's, because that meant we could stop eating Ramen noodles and Hormel Ready to eat meals in a container. While he wasn't working, he was on the chat lines and meeting up with women, because I saw his phone in the bathroom and read the messages. He wasn't concerned about me and his son, and his actions showed that.

I had gotten really sick with food poisoning and he left me in the hotel room with our son, who was sleeping in a playpen, for me to figure it out. I was vomiting non-stop but somehow God gave me strength to take care of our son. I should not have been shocked, because I had already had a glimpse early on the type of parent he would be. He did not care, he had other plans, and taking care of a baby was not in them. I knew what I had been dealing with and it was not going to stop because of the location.

He ended up going back to jail again for driving while suspended. He got out, had a warrant, got out, and committed theft. I knew anytime he was not working, sticky fingers were going to be in action. I had gotten so used to it that I knew when I saw the jail number it was one of the two things. The two charges were reoccurring for him, and he would never go to court, so when he would drive, he'd get caught, and get arrested on outstanding warrants. I ended up back home, singing "Here We Go, Here We Go Again."

The car I got I acquired in a manner I was not supposed to, so it got repossessed. I am sure my parents were sick of me coming back home; however, they didn't want to see me out on the streets, so it was almost like 'until next time' for them, which was coming soon.

Nightmares

When are these dreams going to come off repeat?
I'm running fast & being chased down the street,
strategically plotting my next escape.
I'm hiding with my head on a swivel until I feel safe.
Safe is a feeling that can't seem to settle in.
I close my eyes & then it all happens again.

What is this & why won't it stop?
I feel like I'm losing my mind
& my brain is about to pop.
I'm okay, right? I think so.
I don't want to close my eyes,
because I don't know where my mind will go.
I'm tired of fighting every night in my dreams.
I'm tired of the crying & silent screams,
waking up drenched from the night sweats.

What am I experiencing, because this isn't a test?
My chest is beating fast & I can't catch my breath.
Panic attacks impact my rest—could it be something else?
I escaped a nightmare & still feel like I need some help.
Wake up! Wake Up! The dream is all over.
I beg to differ because the dreams keep getting stronger.

58

CHAPTER 9:
SENTENCING

Chapter 9: Sentencing

In June of 2008, we decided to get married. I was clearly stuck on stupid and parked on dumb. We went and told my parents, and they were nowhere near happy. The face my dad had, and my mom, I could read her thoughts, *this girl has really lost her mind.*

The job I had acquired against my parent's will, he was dropping me off to with a car a member of my parents' church gave us. The car was not in the best shape, but it did what it needed to. I remember while working, he picked me up and was angry with me just because I had him waiting too long. He had one job only and that was to pick me up, yet he was mad because I took too long to come out. I got in the car, and he sped off before I could get in, with my coworkers watching me hanging out the car door. I was so embarrassed, like wow, he did this in front of everyone, and now I must answer all these questions that will follow. He didn't care at all, and I secretly think the shrimp he housed in his pants got a rise out of it.

In March of 2009, while living at the Knights Inn, we got in a huge fight. I was upset because I was the only person working and the clothes that I bought for work he was taking back to Target. He had the audacity to tell me I had no business spending money, yet his unemployed ass was spending all of it. We began arguing and next thing I know he hit me with a left hook. He went all the way Monday Night Raw on me, and what he did next I was not expecting. He picked me up, held me in the air, and dropped me on the floor. He proceeded to beat me like I stole something. He told me to clean my face off, left, and walked to

Chapter 9: Sentencing

Target because we no longer had a car. The car we had was not operating due to the engine and we could not afford to fix it. My dad was picking me up and making sure I was getting to and from work. When he left and went to Target, not only did I go to the front office, but I told them to call Merrillville police, and they did. I contacted my mom and dad and told them to come get me immediately.

I was fleeing yet again, like a criminal that just robbed the bank. I filed the police report and left before he came back. He did not come right back, I was made aware by the officers. He knew instantly what happened and told me when he talked to me that I blew it out of proportion. I ended things with him, and he moved to Shreveport where he was staying with friends. I was glad he had moved so far away. I knew with him being so far away there was no room for reconciliation, and this was my chance to finally be set free.

I started getting my life back on track and my parents saw that I was trying. We went shopping for clothes and I got my hair done. I had developed a pattern similar to those who are released from jail. I would be greeted with open arms, clothes, in hand, and making my appearance better. I had no vehicle so the best option, seeing as the buy here pay car here did not work in the past, was cash. We found a good used old school Buick. I was not being choosy, so my parents got a loan, and I was required to pay them back as I received paychecks. The whole time I was rebuilding I really thought distance would help me get over the relationship, but the truth is it did not. He was back to his old comeback games.

He sent me a pair of Coach shoes because he was finally working and had a job. My mother sarcastically laughed at the gesture and said do not fall for it like the Lolita Lempicka perfume. "Lolita is how he got you the first time."

He was constantly calling, acting concerned, and it kicked up a notch once I got in a car accident. I was hit from behind by a semi-truck after picking my son up from school. The car was totaled, and we had injuries. The only thing he was worried about was did I get an attorney, but I knew what that was about. He was anticipating a big payout for his benefit. I was back to square one, not having a vehicle anymore. We were secretly repairing our relationship, and I continued working. He visited shortly after, and not too many weeks later, he moved back. In the process of him moving back, I ended up buying my mom's friend's vehicle for $2,000. I was happy because it was a nice car. I told my parents that we were going to move back to Indianapolis, and we did.

I stayed connected with my parents when I first got to Indy; however, that would change soon. Life came at me fast, but this was the life I had been accustomed to.

We started staying in an extended stay hotel, where I hated everything about it. The devil did not take long to show me hell because he unpacked his bags and started his devilish ways. He would have me sleeping on the floor of a nasty hotel and would turn the air on because he knew I did not have a cover. I was taking the blow dryer while he was asleep and putting it on my body to keep warm. If you've ever been to a hotel, anybody knows the blower dryer is small. He had not started back physically abusing me, but he was emotionally abusing me. He was telling me that nobody else on this earth wanted me. It was like every time I would go back, he would punish me for leaving. He would never admit to it, but his actions communicated that. I was working for Telamon in Carmel, and he got a job there too, but his background check came back, and he lost the job because he lied. The theft charges and driving while suspended was starting to haunt him. He was back to dropping me off at work while he did whatever he wanted to. We eventually found a townhouse after a few short weeks of being in a hotel, because living in hotels was very expensive. We needed some help, so I enlisted my dad. He was going to get a U-Haul to help us, but my ex did not like the idea. We got in the car, and we were driving down 465 South, arguing. He backhanded me in my face as our son sat in the car seat behind me and told me to never disrespect him again. The help we needed was convenient, we needed it. My dad was just trying to make it easier on us. He told me I could not call them anymore and I had to cut off communication.

We moved in and things were not okay. The clothes could not get good on the hangers before he started clowning. I was not allowed to open blinds in the house, and if I did there was price to pay. He would accuse me of opening them just so he could have an excuse to put his hands on me. I am positive he was the devil's son, because who does not like natural sunlight?

Chapter 9: Sentencing

I remember there was a time he dropped me off at work and my supervisor was outside smoking when we pulled up. He saw me so he came up to the car and spoke to us both. He made me leave work and pulled off in an angry state. He started pushing me in my head, asking me if I thought he was stupid. We argued until we got to the apartment and as soon as we were in the door he started hitting me. He said I was sleeping with my supervisor and said I was not supposed to be wearing jeans to work. We had a dress code, but we could wear non-fitted jeans which I did not do. He took all the pants and jeans I accumulated while staying at my parents' house, put them in the tub, and bleached them all. He stated I would wear dresses like my mother going forward. Yeah, the woman who he could not stand. My mother had flower dresses that reminded you of the show "Blossom," so he was trying to be funny, but nothing was funny at that moment. I stood there, yelling for him to stop while I was crying, but he did not care. He finished, threatened me, and proceeded about his day. I was a no call no show the very next day and I eventually lost that job.

We ended up being in a financial bind because I didn't have a job, so he wanted me to reach out to my parents to ask for money to put on the prepaid phone, and I did. The thing he didn't know was I was secretly emailing my mother all along via email. I was able to find a temp job right down the street from home. He was still doing what he wanted, talking to who he wanted, and dictating my every move. I hated every waking moment at that townhome because so much bad happened there.

Chapter 9: Sentencing

I remember while one day, my son and I, along with him, were sitting in the room watching cartoons. My son was on my lap, and he tried to accuse me of inappropriately touching him. I was like *what?* Are you crazy? You have lost your mind. He lost it and told my son to go in the other room so the devil could work within him. He jumped on me, started slapping me, grabbed me by the neck, and strangled me until I lost consciousness. I came back conscious, and he did it again. I was gasping for air, and he left the room and told me do not come out. I was looking around in disbelief because he had never taken it that far in strangling me to where I blacked out. I was very scared, because I felt like he was trying to kill me. He told me to clean my face and for my son to come back in the room, and he left. A person who thinks someone has caused harm to their child would not leave them with that person period. No matter what the relationship is.

I knew right there he was beyond sick in the head. He came back with food, and he did not get me any. He got my son and himself some, and I had to sit there and watch them eat. I was starving but he did not give a damn. He was playing emotional games to get to me. I noticed he would always make up stuff, like when he told me I didn't clean the kitchen well enough. He said because a pot of spaghetti was still in the refrigerator it was not cleaned. He grabbed the pot, took his hands, and started throwing the spaghetti on the walls like he was an animal. He got in my face, yelling, "You did not clean shit!" and pushed me. I had never seen anything like that in my life. He proceeded to tell me I needed to clean the mess up he had made. He filled a mop bucket up, handed me the mop, and I had to mop the carpet. It had to be the dumbest thing I had heard of to mop the carpet, but this was some weird shit he did regularly on a normal day. I finished mopping the carpet and right after he took the bucket of mop water and dumped it on me. I was drenched, in tears, and questioning my existence. I felt so violated on another level. He left after, like nothing happened.

The craziness didn't end, it just intensified. My niece came over one day and must have been sitting in the cut because he asked if she was over. I told him my niece had been over and the rest went to hell, where he lived. He proceeded to beat me so badly, and after he beat me, I was told to take my clothes off and he pushed me outside naked. Shortly after, he told me to get dressed and drove me to Bainbridge, Indiana in the middle of a corn field. I was directed to get out and acted as if he was going to leave me while my son watched from the back seat. He made me beg him not to leave me out there. I was breaking down inside and I thought I was going to lose it. I was allowed back in the car and told not to ever let anyone in our house ever again or it would be worse. I agreed to do so, and we drove back to Indy. We eventually got kicked out of our apartment because there was a water issue that he felt was not being addressed properly. He complained, they stated they fixed it, and so he didn't like it. He threatened he would withhold the rent, which he did, and they filed an eviction. We were back to trying to figure things out, so this time, we put all our belongings in storage until we moved to a hotel that was right by my job

Chapter 9: Sentencing

I hated that we moved so close because I was afraid my coworkers would start asking questions. He would make me walk to work although we had a car. If we got in an argument, he would not take me to work, and I would have to be a no call no show. I remember he was being an asshole and we were arguing, he made me walk while he drove slow beside the car. It was the most embarrassing thing ever. Mind you, my coworkers were heading in to work so some saw me. I had a few ask, "Where you be coming from?" but I made up a story.

I kept on working, and eventually his stealing ways got him in trouble. He would rather steal than work, so he got arrested for theft twice in one month. I ended up calling my sister to get us out of that hotel. We went to go stay with her, and my assignment had ended. He ended up getting out of jail and wanted to see our son, so I allowed him to do so. He kidnapped him and would not give him back to me. I called my parents immediately, and momma was like, trust me, he does not want that baby. He is doing that to get to you. He tried to make me lose my mind temporarily, and I did. I swear hours felt like days, and I heard the doorbell ring. I don't know who talked to him or what made him change his mind, but he dropped my son back off. He went to jail again for stealing and ended up on work release. I was working, so I made sure to put my son in daycare at my job because life did not stop for me because of his situation. I continued living with my sister until he got out of work release. He got out, we reconciled, and we ended up back in a hotel.

Chapter 9: Sentencing

CHAPTER 10:
POST-TRIAL

He made promises to get a job; however, it was not fulfilled. He did more job searching while in work release than he did the whole decade I knew him because he just wanted that time away from the facility. We moved to another extended stay hotel, which became our home for quite some time, actually, a few months. I was shelling out tons and tons of money to pay, but we were there so long we started paying monthly.

We were still arguing but we were not fighting. He was still controlling when it came to money, as I did not have access. He would sit outside the hotel and stay in the car for hours while being on the phone. He had told me he would stop smoking weed, yet I would find the trees where he thought he cleaned up. I also would find the remnants floating in the toilet. He was just a habitual liar, so he believed his own lies, but I knew better. I would watch him leave us for hours at a time in a hotel. It was so hard just going to work and coming back to a room with no outside activities. I missed my family so much, and I was depressed.

I noticed one day while getting something out of the trunk that he had brand new clothes. He was going out and enjoying life while I was in captivity. I was so over it, but the thing that made me over it the most was an argument that ensued. I was ready for my son to go to school because my mother put me in school at the age of three. I asked him if he would just work anywhere just to help me make sure our son was able to go to school. He said he wasn't going to work at Walmart or just anywhere. Hell, Walmart would not hire him if he was the last man on earth with all those charges. He had more charges than a Discover, AMEX, Visa, and Master card. We started arguing, and that is when it all clicked for me. I was not about to shortchange my child on his education because he wanted to be a bum. The rubber had met the road, and I was at my breaking point.

The very next day he got arrested for stealing yet again. I tell you, God has a funny way of working. I got the phone call and instantly had to figure out what my next move was. I knew something was off because he was supposed to bring food back and never returned. I knew the routine of him being arrested, so I had to make things happen quick. I had to think on my feet, so I developed a plan and called my mom to come get my son because they were in town. God was looking out of for me by placing my parents in town at that time. I had no money or car because my car was towed and held on a detective hold, so they gave me bus money. I was not about to be around that hotel feeling sorry for myself. I tightened my bootstraps up and got on the bus in the dark while knowing my baby was safe. I went to work like nothing was going on because nobody there knew I was in a tumultuous situation. I got off work, packed that hotel room up, and left. I knew I was done, so my parents paid off the remaining balance, because once again they did not want me with that burden. I went to stay with my sister yet again until I could figure life out.

The phone calls started rolling in and he wanted me to put money on the phone so he could call. I did but with intentions of being an asshole. I turned the phone on, and all the text messages started coming through. I dropped to my knees while reading those messages. The women were going off asking him where their money was and that they had kids to feed. The kicker was that I found out the day he was arrested he was headed to Cincinnati later to meet a woman he was talking to. She was in church and thought she met a saint, but little did she know she met Lucifer's son. She was texting his phone and I was replying as if I was his sister. I let her know where he was, how she could reach him, and that he would look forward to hearing from her. I was done with him, so I did not want him. I was a wife that was sick of an abusive, manipulative individual and was willing to get him off my hands and into someone else's.

I look back on that moment and I am not proud of it, but it is the truth that I need to release. He called the phone by using someone else's minutes to talk to me. I relayed that I saw the text messages and his women were reaching out. I told him it was over that very moment. There was nothing to further talk about, because my mind was made up the prior day after the discussion about or son's education.

The phone calls and letters kept coming in after that conversation. He was trying to get me back in any way he could. He was livid, and he sent a copy of the divorce in a letter to me and wrote "Love." I said oh, he's crazy for real, he thinks this is a game, but the only one who was being played was him.

Chapter 10: Post-Trial

Paranoia

I can't stop feeling the way I'm feeling.
I look over my shoulder like a person in the store stealing.

I see shadows of silhouettes that fit your description.
I feel like I need to see a doctor so they can write a prescription.

I walk across the street & check the mirrors constantly.
I wait to get out of the car, because I fear something happening to me.

I keep reminding myself that I'm finally free.
Somehow, feeling free is just too foreign to me.

I can't shake this feeling. I know something is wrong.
The feeling was valid because I pulled up & he was waiting for me to get home.

How did he know where I lived? I concealed that in every way possible.
He must've followed me to the daycare & home because he felt unstoppable.

In a car, trying to lay low like my spirit wouldn't know.
I'm glad I spotted him before I opened the car door.

Chapter 10: Post-Trial

//

I put my car in reverse & tried to stay calm.
I made a phone call without trying to make him alarmed.

I was slowly being followed while he thought I wouldn't know.
I pulled into a safe place where I *knew* he wouldn't go.

He decided to park across the street like he had all the power.
He tried to intimidate me by calling my phone & acting like a coward.

He was cursing me out & trying to make me feel afraid.
This was the day he found out I was no longer his slave.

CHAPTER 11:
rELEASE DATE

Chapter 11: Release Date

On October 24, 2011, I completed an 8 ½ year sentence. The judge signed off on the divorce paperwork, and I was no longer legally or mentally in bondage. I did not walk away with the things I went in with, but I walked away with something more valuable. I came out with my mind, limbs, health, and, most importantly, my child. I was stripped of everything, but that was as my mother would say just "stuff." I wanted nothing from him, not even child support, because he would never work long enough to obtain money, so it was a waste of time. He was given visitation rights when he got out of jail, but we all knew jail was his real home. I just wanted to be able to keep my car and any association of my maiden's name. The crazy thing is, I never made a name change, because I knew it was not permanent or forever. I only used that name to put on my divorce paperwork because I did not know what I was doing. I just did not want any hiccups.

I hollered down the street as I left the courtroom because I was no longer a prisoner, and I was finally free. I was free in my heart and free in my mind, and freedom—you cannot put a price on that. I called my mother and I cried. I did not care who saw me rejoicing because they could not relate to the joy I had. I was able to start living, because I had been only existing. I was yelling, "Thank You, Jesus, I am Free!" The burden, the blood, the bruises, the beat-up credit, the brokenness, the embarrassment, the shame, I could finally walk away from it all.

I continued staying with my sister, and when he was finally released from jail that winter, he reached out to me. He wanted to retrieve his belongings, so I met him to give them to him. I told one person about what I was doing because I had no fear. I saw him, I knew I was no longer scared, and I realized the fear was removed when freedom was activated. He must have still thought I was playing because he was trying to make passes and I declined. He saw his son and we left, but that didn't stop him from reaching out to see if I would turn back to my old ways. He would send songs to me and send messages on Facebook, and I had to put him in his place because that chapter was closed.

Chapter 11: Release Date

CHAPTER 12: PAROLE

Chapter 12: Parole

My son and I were in a safe place. I started to get my life back to what I thought was on track. I was repairing relationships with everyone, including my best friend/cousin. I was just ready to enjoy life and enjoy the things I once did not. I jumped into dating quicker than I thought I would, but it turned out being the best thing that happened to me. The newfound relationship kept me very distracted and helped in my process of discovering the new me. He was a breath of fresh and was patient with me and accepted all my flaws. I was loved properly in the process of turning into the victor and not the victim. I did not know that after moving on and starting a new relationship that I was still going to have drama. I thought I was going to have some peace. However, I was being stalked in the process.

I was being followed, because my ex-husband went up to my son's school. I had not communicated anything to him about his school at all however he showed up with two bags of hot Cheetos. I was livid because here he goes showing up to the same school, he did not want to fund at all. I got a phone call about why I was letting my new boyfriend pick him up, as if I was not a grown woman but also a person who would never put my child in a dangerous situation ever again. I was baffled because of the audacity but more so because they had no clue how long I knew him, but that was not their business, and I did not owe an explanation. I argued while standing in the hallway at work, trying not to draw any attention to myself. I let that school know to never ever let him come to the school.

Chapter 12: Parole

The very same week I was headed home and lo and behold I saw someone sitting in the cut of my boyfriend's apartment complex. I was not scared, but I was very aware of my surroundings, especially after he pulled that stunt. I spotted it was him he because his hat sat low on his eyes that sank in the back of his head. I called my boyfriend as I was backing out and his job was less than two minutes away. I relayed what was happening while driving and he asked where I was, I said about to pull up and he came out the door. He waved at him as he drove past and went and parked across the street and sat in the car while we argued on the phone. I could not deal with him anymore.

He thought he still had power, but that cord had been disconnected. I told him I would call the police because he was stalking me. He eventually left but he stated to me that he saw me having sex with the lights on and I told him I hoped he enjoyed the show. It was in that moment I knew he had been watching for quite some time. The very next day there were nails in my tire. The way they were positioned, a nail gun was utilized, and I knew it was nobody but him. He forgot that I witnessed him in earlier days slash tires with a knife. I called him and let him have it, because now he was going in my pockets, but of course he denied it, because that's what liars do. He eventually left me alone only because I am sure he got locked up again for having sticky fingers.

I proceeded on with life, but I noticed there were some things I did not like about myself, and others were pointing it out. I had some aggressive ways, something that I never was. My boyfriend would always say, "Why are you always hitting me in my arm?" I was doing it in a joking manner, but he didn't think anything was funny. I was always very jumpy when someone would get too close to me or in my personal space, and I would tense up and flinch. I was told by others that this was what I was doing, I had some underlying issues that no man, woman, or any family could help me with, and I had to make the healthy decision to seek additional assistance. I was having nightmares and night sweats for years after the divorce, and it put me in a paralyzing state. I thought the fear was gone, but in fact it was more present than what I tried to trick my mind into believing. I had booby traps set up in my home because I made a vow to myself not to be physically hurt again. I started my journey of finding a counselor, then I reached out to an agency that provided free services.

CHAPTER 13: REHABILITATION

October 2016, I began going to free counseling at Families First to deal and heal. I not only got healing for myself but for my son as well. He started displaying some negative behaviors and they needed to be addressed immediately. He had a fuse and an incident with my youngest son and nephew took place and he went into protect mode, not identifying that my nephew was just a little toddler and was not trying to hurt his little brother. He was livid and started crying and going off and that is when I knew we had an issue to address. I knew that within myself I needed some healing, and the reality of my son's situation was mine as well.

We were able to identify that I had triggers and I never healed from that relationship. I walked away but I never got the help I needed. I had experienced trauma and I thought by getting divorced, getting remarried, and living all that would cover the trauma. The trauma became apparent, as the exercises we did pulled out things I was internalizing. I did not like certain colognes because when he would slap me, I would smell it on his hands. I hated riding past the hotels we lived in, I was looking over my shoulder, and so many more. We worked diligently to make sure that I started my healing journey. The combination of the individual and the group healing really helped me. The group helped me because I was the only woman in the class who had their child at home. The other women were there because the kids were removed from the home. I cried the first day I went to group counseling when I got in the car. I didn't even know or think that could have happened to me. I had God's grace on my side that nobody ever called, because my baby would have been taken from me. The women in that class had to have supervised visits, and here I am, picking up my child from the next room on the way out the door. It broke me down, but it put things into perspective.

I was able to help them and let them know they could get out and stay out. I did not want to graduate from that class, but it was time for me to walk in true freedom. The day I completed those classes is the day I began to live again.

ABOUT THE AUTHOR

C. Nicole is a wife and mother of two boys, ages seven and fifteen. She currently resides in Indianapolis, IN, and is a licensed insurance agent. In her spare time, she enjoys spending time with her family and friends, skating, dancing, blogging, writing poetry, and researching.